PRAISE FOR A BOOK OF WOMEN'S ALTARS
ALSO BY NANCY BRADY CUNNINGHAM AND DENISE GEDDES

"Reading this book, ancient memories are stirred of a time when women paid tribute to seasons and life cycles by creating indoor and outdoor altars. *A Book of Women's Altars* is beautifully written and filled with many specific suggestions. The photographs encourage the reader to breathe a bit more deeply. In both the images and the words, there is a fresh simplicity, a lack of pretense and a reclaiming of the original intention of altars, which was to express awareness of the sacredness of all life."

—Gloria D. Karpinski, author of *Barefoot on Holy Ground* and *Where Two Worlds Touch*

"A fresh and innovative exploration of prayer and sacredness in our everyday life. This book is its own 'ritual of the heart.'"

—Lynn Andrews, author of *Medicine Woman* and *Tree of Dreams*

"A perfect balance of evocative photography and inviting prose, this book illustrates how easy and essential it is for women to create sacred spaces to honor their visions, concerns, and desires."

—Dana Carpenter, co-founder, Sole Sisters Inc. and editor of *I am Beautiful*

"*A Book of Women's Altars* is worship, magic, artistry, and passion. The ancient art of creating altars is preserved and expanded in this beautiful book. The exquisite words and photographs of Nancy Brady Cunningham and Denise Geddes inspire us to create a physical connection to the sacred in our own lives."

—Louisa and Rick Clerici, authors of *Sparks from the Fire of Time*

"A book like this is long overdue and applicable to a life-long spiritual journey. The list of uses for a personal altar is a welcome reminder for anyone; the definitions of "altar" expand one's possibilities for honoring, growing, and celebrating. I have many altars in my home and office and recommend them in my books, but here for the first time is an exhaustive exploration and focus on the subject with contemporary touchstones and rationale."

—Jennifer Bosveld, Director of Pudding House Writers' Innovation Center

"A lovely, poetic guide to inviting the sacred into our everyday lives."

—Kris Waldherr, author of *The Goddess Tarot* and *Sacred Animals*

"A visually evocative and inspirational book—gives women an opportunity to create their own spiritual sanctuaries."

—Dan & Marty Campanelli, Flying Witch Farm

"This book shares a wonderful vision for creating sacred space in your life—each altar and ritual can change everyday into beauty."

—Amy Zerner, artist and author of *Love, Light, and Laughter*; *Oracle of the Goddess*; and *Gifts of the Goddess*

"*A Book of Women's Altars* by Nancy Cunningham is a marvelously creative and helpful book which helps us bring the creative symbolic world and the haven of spirit together in the everyday corners of our lives. Denise Geddes's photographs shows diverse altars so we may better create altars by which to dream and pray."

—Janell Moon, author of *The Wise Earth Speaks to Your Spirit* and *Stirring the Waters*

"What a profound spirituality of awareness Nancy Brady Cunningham gives in her wise and beautiful practice of making altars. Suddenly I see opportunities for altars at every intersection of creation with Divine Mystery. She helps me realize that the altars I've made since childhood are centerpieces of my spiritual practice; a meeting place for all that is deepest in my soul. Every flower is an opportunity, each stone and feather, every fallen leaf. Every woman needs this book!"

—Christin Lore Weber, author of *Altar Music*, *Womanchrist*, and *Circle of Mysteries*

"Nancy Brady Cunningham's book offers a lovely invitation to create meditative spaces of your own for clarity and well-being. Her guidelines are inspiring and creative and encourage you to combine natural elements with personal treasures."

—Hailey D.D. Klein, author of *The Way of Change: Finding Joy in Your Journey*

"This book is a haiku of a guide that allows your inner wisdom out to play. I have always made altars and yet to make them consciously, for a purpose, that has eluded me. I will use this practical invitation."

—Jennifer Louden, author of *The Woman's Retreat Book* and *The Comfort Queen's Guide to Life*

Snow

Melting

in a

SILVER BOWL

A Book of Active Meditations

Nancy Brady Cunningham
and Denise Geddes

Red Wheel
Boston, MA / York Beach, ME

Handwritten inscription:

For Tom,
With fondness
& appreciation
for your
Poetry &
Parenthood.

Peace

Bob & Jim

Christmas,
2013

First published in 2004 by
Red Wheel/Weiser, LLC
York Beach, ME
With offices at:
368 Congress Street
Boston, MA 02210
www.redwheelweiser.com

Library of Congress Cataloging-in-Publication Data

Cunningham, Nancy Brady
Snow melting in a silver bowl : a book of active meditations /
Nancy Brady Cunningham ; photography by Denise Geddes.
     p. cm.
Includes bibliographical references.
   ISBN 1-59003-063-X (alk. paper)
 I. Meditation. I. Geddes, Denise. II. Title.
   BL627.C86 2004
   204'.35--dc22
                                    2004004147

Typeset in Matrix by Anne Carter

Printed in the United States
Malloy

11 10 09 08 07 06 05 04
   8 7 6 5 4 3 2 1
The paper used in this publication meets the minimum requirements of the American National Standard
for Information Sciences-Permanence of Paper for Printed Library Materials Z39.48-1992 (R1997).

Contents

Foreword

There are some books that, as you read them, cause the boundary between the eternal now and current reality to thin. Your breath deepens, your eyes soften, your jaw loosens. As you read, you are drawn into winged palaces of heightened clarity, glossy unfoldings of possibility, an endless horizon of wisdom.

For me, Nancy and Denise have created such a book. Reading these meditations and seeing these photographs, I am lit with the fire I need to draw me toward God. I am a spiritual pilgrim who, I confess, is easily distracted. My internal conversation can ramble on something like, "Why go to yoga? Why go to church? A nap is a spiritual practice. So is eating chocolate. C'mon, just lay your head down." More pernicious is the chatter that hisses, "Creating and helping others wake up is all fine and good but only if it makes truckloads of money." It is in these desolate moments that I need my spiritual fire relit, I need help returning to the still center, to the part of me that knows there is only one mind, one taste, one purpose.

I am grateful to add to my tool box these intimate offerings of dramatized prayer. Like the tongue of a bell pealing or a trail of bird tracks in wet sand, these prayers call me back to what is true.

May you find restoration and grace as you make these ideas part of your spiritual practice. It is so easy to practice the petty and to subsist in self-exile. For some strange reason, too often, this is the direction we are pulled in. I am filled with such gratitude that we also have ideas and images such as these to tug us back to the source.

Jennifer Louden
Bainbridge Island, Washington
2003

Preface

This is a nonbook. Rather than disseminating information, I hope to share a sense of wonder! Toward that end I have used poetic language, a measured rhythm, a vocabulary sprinkled with near rhymes, and word pools that create visions in the mind.

In spite of my attempts, the book evokes no magic without the photographs. Denise Geddes's sensitive images manifest the radiance hidden within our everyday world, making the light within all things visible. *Snow Melting in a Silver Bowl* becomes a gift from Denise and me to all people who wish to bring the unity of the underlying life force into sharper focus.

Acknowledgments

Nancy:

Loving thanks to Denise Geddes for her patience in transforming my hen-scratching into neatly typed pages! And for putting the entire manuscript on the computer—a skill I envy!

Warm thanks to my circle sisters—our group rituals are a constant inspiration to me.

I owe a great debt of thanks to everyone in the Poetry Workshop at the Boston Center for Adult Education, with special gratitude to Ottone M. Riccio, who facilitates the workshop with warmth and humor.

I'm grateful to my husband Ed for sharing his knowledge and enthusiasm for Mother Nature and all things natural. My loving appreciation to Cara and Rob and grandchildren Alex, Lily, and Lucy; to Devin and Missy and grandchildren Kelsey and Devin.

Denise:

Many thanks to Mike Morin for allowing me to photograph his wonderful assortment of musical instruments for this book. Similar gratitude to Infinity Books, New Bedford, Massachusetts, for letting me take pictures in the store.

Gratitude and love to Nancy Brady Cunningham for involving me in this wonderful project.

Loving thanks to my mother for rescuing me when camera disaster struck mid-project, and to Jason Geddes for helping me figure out what to do next. I am blessed indeed!

Thank you to my children, my siblings, and my community at Sudbury Valley School for all the encouragement and support I receive. It is bountiful!

VISIONS TAKING FORM:

What is active meditation?

AT FIRST BLUSH the phrase "active meditation" may well seem a contradiction in terms. The juxtapositioning of "active," an adjective suggesting lively, dynamic, bustling behavior, with the word "meditation," a noun indicating a kind of contemplative reflection that necessitates physical stillness, produces a phrase that seems implausible. Meditation is considered by many to be a mental process, although in its purest form it is actually a state of "nonthought," a step inward to the realm of pure awareness. Meditation begins with quieting the mind—the "monkey mind" as it is called in yoga philosophy. Monkey mind refers to surface mind: the tape that runs incessantly in your head; the mind that is prone to anxiety and fear; the mind that ceases to settle anywhere for long; the mind that embroiders an emotional response onto the most routine, mundane, bland happenings; the mind that, with blinding speed, finds a way to escape the "here and now." That mind! The friendly enemy that scoffs at the peace, quiet, and calm of the deeper mind, assuring you that such qualities are vastly overrated.

If the goal of meditation is to journey into the deeper mind, wouldn't activity work in opposition to that goal? Wouldn't sitting quietly be more beneficial in order to allow your awareness to deepen into a meditative state, to slip below the siren call of the emotions, to move inward to a place where you are not rattled by the racket of the world?

Not necessarily! Actions can be slowed to a pace that permits the mind to fully attend to the active meditation. Pulling the mind to one point in order to be completely present during an activity calms the monkey mind and allows one to visit the peaceful realm that exists just below the surface mind. It is this shift of consciousness, brought about through active meditation, that soothes the mind away from its excited state into a profound place of quiet serenity. Actions *can* speak in soft tones that gather the scattered mind to a central point, then gentle the mind's focus inward.

Active meditation begins with the introduction of an activity that absorbs the monkey mind; it can be exquisitely simple: lighting a candle that is placed before a photo of your grandmother as part of a "day of the dead" celebration in honor of your ancestors. Or active meditation can be as complex as the Japanese tea ceremony. Both contain actions performed with a spirit of reverence and a profound concentration.

The physicality of the action, in and of itself, does not create the connection to meditative realms. It is the level of concentrated awareness that creates the shift in consciousness. Absent-mindedness could lead to a scorched photo, burnt fingers, or flaming hair, or in the second example spilt tea, scalded fingers, or broken cups. Activity that requires focusing, which, in turn, slows your movements and allows you to simultaneously be in the activity and in your deeper self, constitutes the first ingredient of active meditation.

The second is intention. In the ancestor example, acknowledgment of the debt owed to "those who came before" strikes a chord of gratitude in the heart, and thus, an appreciative salute to your origins is the intent. In the tea example, honoring the guest, and thus simultaneously paying homage to the inner divine self, becomes the intention.

The spirit of active meditation comes into sharper focus when you look over a list of other terms used to designate "active meditation":

Ceremony

Rite

Ritual

Celebration

Observance

Tangible visualization

Dramatized prayer

Although in religious or liturgical parlance these words are not interchangeable (for example, in Native American lore, the word "ceremony" constitutes a specific form of ritual), for the general purposes of this volume these terms will be used interchangeably.

Active meditation does not stand in direct opposition to seated meditation; rather, one may be used as a prelude to the other. In the ancestor ritual, the candle lighting might be a prelude to a grateful heart meditation, in which you sit quietly with eyes closed and concentrate on your heartbeat. Send vibrations of gratitude out into the universe toward your ancestors and beyond, picturing yourself in a long line of women trailing back to the beginnings of time, with thankfulness in your heart toward all.

In the tea ritual, you might begin with a simple "counting the breaths" meditation for twenty minutes to center yourself before performing the ceremony.

Active meditation and classic meditation are strands of different-colored yarn that can both be woven into your meditation blanket.

1

COMMUNING WITH THE DEEPER SELF:

Why create an active meditation?

ritual

prayers painted
on scented water
overflow the altar bowl
where half-drenched letters
rise up in blurry alphabets—
mouth the dazzle

ACTIVE MEDITATIONS may be viewed as rituals of intention. Why not simply keep your intentions alive in your mind and heart? In essence, this is the first step in creating a simple ceremony—deciding on a heart-felt reason to perform the active meditation. Ritual then moves beyond the abstract into the physical realm, due to the awareness that the deep mind reveals itself in the language of symbols.

Much time and money are spent in consulting psychologists concerning the interpretations of dreams, nightmares, visions, body language, art-work, children's play therapy, and Jungian sand-tray therapy. There seems to be widespread agreement in psychology that the deeper mind (the other 95 percent of the iceberg) sends messages to the conscious mind by means of symbols. In active meditation, symbolic language is used to communicate our intentions to the deep mind, thus making a conversation out of what was once a monologue.

Sophy Burnham, in her book about angels[1], offers the reader a way to pray effectively. One step is to visualize your prayer request as a *fait accompli*. This envisioning speaks to the deep mind in a way that words alone do not; in addition, seeing the intention as a "done deal" brings it into reality more quickly. In active meditation, even this visualization process is taken a step further—you enact your intention. This enactment requires two things: a symbol of one of the four elements and the involvement of one of your five senses. The deep mind is profoundly connected with the natural world, so your senses and the elements speak to that interconnectedness. Each person is a microcosm composed of nature's elements: Air (breath), Fire (energy), Water (blood), and Earth (body). Another link is the appeal to at least one of the senses because sights, smells, sounds, tastes, and touch bring us into the present moment; in the deep mind, time and space do not exist—there is only the eternal now.

In active meditation, you open the conversation by centering on an intention, continue by choosing a prop (or more than one) that represents an element, then intensify the communication through an appeal to one of your five senses. With these three steps, your intention becomes tangible, and you have enlivened your intent with a universal energy that brings about a change in consciousness, a shift in perception, an altered state.

The ceremonies run the gamut of human experience; for example, any intention for which you might offer prayers could become an active meditation that is, in essence, a dramatized prayer. A bedtime petition for protection through the night could evolve into an incense blessing for your bedroom.

LIGHT A STICK OF INCENSE. Slowly walk around your room, slipping the smoke over all your favorite things: books, crystals, plants, photos, and clothing. Turn out the light and walk once around your bed, the glow from the tip creating a circle of light and protection for you as you sleep. Place the incense stick in a holder. Reverently set it before a picture or statue of the divine, such as Buddha, Blessed Mary, an angel, a goddess, or the earth mother. Drift off to dreamland knowing that the smoke continues to send protection prayers to the powers that be. When you awaken the next morning, the lingering scent will call you to morning meditation.

A THANKSGIVING DAY CELEBRATION can be enhanced through an unusual toast. Give each person a goblet of water and ask everyone, in turn, to raise their glass in honor of one person they are grateful to, and to share the reason they feel thankful for this person's presence in their life. When all have had their say, rather than taking a sip, ask folks to pour the water into a punch bowl, one person at a time. Silence should prevail so that all can hear each person's splash of thanksgiving. The hostess then stirs the contents saying, "We mingle our thanks as we gather here today, joining our spirits as one." Then she ladles out a glass of thankfulness to each person; everyone clinks glasses and sips, completing the toast.

A NAMING CEREMONY FOR A NEWBORN could begin with guests forming a circle of love around parents and baby. While the mother distributes a flower to each guest, the father shares the meaning of the child's name and their reasons for choosing that name for their child. The baby is then handed around the circle, and each guest offers a blessing for the baby, while stroking the newborn's cheek with the flower. The mother ends with, "Our newborn will be called _____ from this day forward. May our circle of blessings follow him (her) all the days of his (her) life." The mother gathers up the flowers and places them in a vase beside the bassinet or crib; the baby will sleep amid a shower of fragrant blessings.

ON A DAY WHEN YOU FEEL SCATTERED, this ritual can help you collect the pieces. Sound is arresting—it pulls your awareness to the present. Percussive sounds, in their purity and intensity, rapidly transport you to that focused center behind all the worry, aggravation, and stress of your day.

Bring the mind (Air) into clarity by ringing a crystal wineglass or bowl. Retrieve your physical energy (Fire) by erasing fatigue with a heartbeat rhythm played on a small drum. Calm your emotions (Water) with the metallic sound of a bell or gong, rung with the slow, stately grace of a church bell. Clack two pieces of wood or stone (Earth) together; feel the vibrations traveling up your arms, revitalizing your entire body. End by chanting the syllable Om (rhymes with home), the primordial sound, the alpha and omega of all sound in the universe. Chant until you feel quiet inside.

THE PHRASE "LETTING GO" tends to create mild apprehension in many people because it suggests loss. Consider that there are some things in your life that you could lose and not miss them one iota. Dwell on the ways in which such a letting go would free you. Contemplate the space you would create by ridding yourself of a dead-end job, an avocation that no longer interests you, a membership in a club you've outgrown.

Write what you are willing to sacrifice on a piece of looseleaf paper. Crumple it. Place it in a fireproof container and light it, while saying aloud, "I am letting go of _____. Now I have more time for activities that nourish me." Let your full attention center on the flames as you watch the paper shrink to a few ashes. Scatter the ashes to the four winds, knowing that you have created an open space where a new blessing may enter your life.

Since the language of the deeper mind is symbols, it is, for all intents, deaf to verbiage. Much like the hearing-impaired person who never learned to read lips, the deep mind yearns for the clear, precise, economical gestures of the sign language that is called ritual.

2

HARMONIC RESONANCE:

Entwining classic meditation techniques with active meditation

communion

throated lilies
open to
threads of silver rain
perfuming
the holy

THROUGH THE ADDITION OF AN ACTIVITY that calls to the elements and your senses, any classic meditation technique can be transformed into an active meditation. Also, classic meditation can be used to begin an active meditation; conversely, a ritual ceremony can be used to settle your mind before a quiet-sitting meditation.

There are some differences, however, between the two types of meditation. Meditation, in its purest form, seeks to transcend the world, the body, and day-to-day existence. Active meditation sees the spiritual within the physical realm, considering all of existence to be holy, sacred, divine. Also, meditation intends to bring the practitioner to a state of pure awareness, an "at-one-ment" with a higher consciousness, a state of bliss arrived at through an inward focus. Active meditation, with its focus on the external, begins with a specific intention: a healing, a celebration of the seasons, a rite of passage. Meditation, in its purest form, seeks enlightenment. Active meditation seeks the spirit in all creation. Both, however, have as their goal connecting the practitioner with a universal energy source; thus, the two can be intertwined in enlightening ways.

MEDITATION FOCUSES ON THE BREATH. Create an active meditation by gathering together a lit candle and a small glass bowl of water. Turn down the lights and with each exhalation breathe out through the mouth, lightly ruffling the water. Candlelight creates a soothing atmosphere. Watching the breath ripple the water's surface allows the invisible to become manifest. Count to five for the inhalation, and then again for the exhalation. Let the busy mind float over the water until it quiets, until there is only the breath. This ritual becomes a literal "watching the breath" meditation.

ANOTHER CLASSIC MEDITATION focuses on the screen of the mind: visualizing light, a visual symbol (for example, the rose), or a realized being. The idea of visualizing a flower can become more tangible through the active meditation of becoming the flower.

Crouch down on the floor or outdoors on the grass. Imagine that you are a seed. Close your eyes and see the seed breaking open; watch green shoots appear. Begin to move. What type of flower are you destined to be? Feel the sun-warmed earth around you, encouraging your growth. You are kneeling now. Lift your arms (shoots) to poke through the topsoil. Warm rains and spring sunlight alternately bless you. Rise up to a standing position. Open your arms wide; reach for the sky. As you unfold your bud, what colors grace your petals and center? Feel the breeze gently fluffing your petals. Let your scent perfume the landscape.

Open your eyes as you slowly bring your arms to your sides. Experience yourself as a fresh new bloom. Carry that awareness into your day.

USING A MANTRA is another traditional meditation technique. Although classically the mantra is given by a guru, you need not adhere to this formality. A mantra can be any words that seem spiritually uplifting to you: a line of poetry, a verse from scripture, a phrase from a prayer, lyrics from a song—whatever you find inspirational.

For active meditation you might combine the words with a gesture: "I warm my heart at heaven's fire" will take on a ritualistic flavor if you light a candle, warm your hands at the flame, bring them to your heart. The repetition of the movement along with the words enlarges the mantra by bringing it into the physical realm.

ANOTHER MANTRA ACTIVITY is written mantra. While saying the words, write them in a journal, allowing them to penetrate deeply into your being.

CANDLEGAZING IS BOTH AN INNER AND OUTER MEDITATION. This technique consists of looking at the flame, then closing your eyes and trying to see the flame in your mind's eye. The concentration needed to envision the flame quiets the chatter of your surface mind. To give candlegazing a physical dimension, look at the flame until you see the halo around the flame. Then, light a stick of incense and move the smoke over your body's halo or aura. End by gazing at the flame while trying to feel the glow of your personal energy as it extends beyond your body, creating a halo. You and the flame become one! All living things possess auras, for the universal life force cannot be contained within contours; rather, it spills beyond the shape of things, forming the interconnectedness of all life.

Once you've chosen your intention, as well as the element and the sense you will use to bring your intention "into the flesh," you are ready to begin. Ritual is a form of consecrated action that focuses the spirit, bestowing a blessing on your dreams and desires. Any classic meditation can be braided in with the ritual elements to create a blended pattern that honors both.

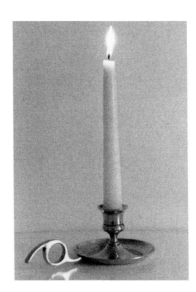

3

cabin

rain drips
through the roofplanks
into my
oatmeal

ACTIVE MEDITATION centers on simple ceremonies to honor the spiritual energy inherent in all life. This form of meditation becomes the link between your interior and exterior lives, allowing a balance to exist between the two. By channeling meditative attention onto an external object or being or experience, you are able to erase the boundaries that keep the inner and outer selves separate. In our culture, one tends to identify the "spiritual" as the "invisible." Active meditation permits the discovery of the radiant soul in all things—plants, people, animals, earth, the elements. Even the apparently inanimate possesses a hidden-within-reach splendor.

ALL MEDITATION REQUIRES A SHIFT in consciousness; however, many traditional forms center on a quiet-sitting type of meditation, in which the practitioner focuses inward on the breath, the heartbeat, a visualization, or a mantra. Active meditation involves an active "doing," for example walking, gesturing, candle lighting, smudging, chanting, or performing a simple chore. Any of these activities, coupled with an inner focusing, can bring about expanded awareness. For example, if you were preparing lunch for a friend who is ill, you could pull the meal together with all the "feeling" of a short-order cook at the local diner during the noon rush.[2] Or you could transform your cooking into an act of prayer by slowing your gestures and meditatively selecting ingredients, then chopping, stirring, slicing, and spreading them with thoughts of mixing light or blessings or healing into the food. Keep your heart open, pouring love into the mix. In the same manner, a quietly attentive mind set can transform any activity into an act of meditation.

ANOTHER KITCHEN CONTEMPLATION involves a transfiguration that begins with the flip of a switch. One evening when you are alone, turn off all the kitchen lights and illuminate the room with candles. Look with "new" eyes at its shapes, hues, and textures—view your kitchen as you

would a piece of found art. The soft flicker of flames allows you to see the hidden beauty as the room metamorphoses into a haven of calm and serenity. Gone is the oven screaming to be scoured, the floor whining to be washed, the piles of clutter begging to be shelved. Candlelight is forgiving! Grease spots on the stove magically vanish, dust on windowsills disappears, curtains (no longer white) take on a lovely cream color in the soft light. The untidy kitchen has become a space for meditation.

Choose one candle, and holding it, walk around the kitchen silently blessing all who gather there for meals. You are encircling the kitchen with the light of love. As you create this circle of light, note that your breathing deepens, the constant chatter of the mind quiets, and you are drawn inward to the stillness place. In this way, active meditation creates a mental state where inner and outer worlds interface. A lit candle in a messy kitchen can reveal how the spirit world lies encircled by the physical realm.

MAKING THE SHIFT AWAY from the workaday mind into a more contemplative state can be enhanced by performing a rite of cleansing. The word "cleansing" does not imply that you are unworthy, unclean, or tainted. Instead, the word applies to the conscious mind—the "monkey mind" that swings unceasingly from one subject to the next, chattering gibberish all the while. The purification acts as a signal to the deep mind that it is time to surface, and to the surface mind that it is time to quiet. A purification suggests, "I am shedding my everyday state of consciousness. I am washing away the linear view of my world so that I might see the immeasurable spirituality all around me." The cleansing is a washing clean of your state of mind so that the mundane may morph into the profound in the fresh light of meditation. Through a purification you create a psychic (soul) space in which to enact the meditation.

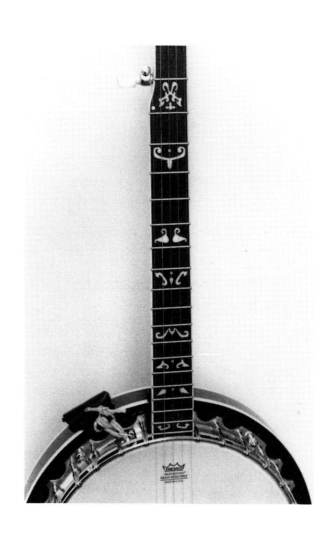

JUST AS THE SINGER PRACTICES SCALES, the musician tunes his instrument, the dancer stretches her body, so too you can prepare the mind-body for the performance of an active meditation[3]:

- Drink a glass of cool spring water. Witness the sensation of the liquid in your mouth, and moving down your throat.

- Wash your hands and face with an aromatic soap, letting the scent calm you.

- Inhale the fragrance of a bundle of fresh herbs; the herbs are eye pleasing and aromatically potent.

- Cleanse your aura by sweeping the bundle from head to toe and around the back of your body. Hold the herb bundle an inch or two out from your body so that you are moving it over the aura (halo) that surrounds your physical self.

- Anoint yourself with essence oil.

- Inhale the scent of an essence oil while seeing healing white light entering your body with each breath. The scent adds a certain physicality to the light and enhances the healing.

These purifications all involve the senses, because the senses are powerful allies in arresting the harried mind, bringing it to one point, and holding it there—the senses bring you into a state of "hereness."

Any purification cleanses the mind of distraction, preoccupation, and the residue of tension from your daily cares. It gathers the mind inward so it may focus on "being" rather than the hectic "doing" of the world.

The spiritual and the physical move through and around each other. You need not divorce yourself from the physical world in order to meditate; active meditation uses the physical plane to reveal the spiritual nature of the most commonplace things. The world is infused with spirit, but divine promptings are subtle; the rituals help create spaces where the divine can be "heard."

4

SIMPLE CEREMONIES:

A path into the realm

of the spirit

ceremony

snow
 melting
  in
   a
  silver
  bowl

ACTIVE MEDITATION can embrace any aspect of your life and need not be time-consuming or elaborate.

The first of the three simple ceremonies in this chapter centers on a celebration of the oneness between mother and child. During infancy, baby and mother arise in the night for that ancient ritual called "middle-of-the-night feedings." Rather than flipping on the television or radio to keep you company during the dead of night, consider these midnight hours as a perfect opportunity for sharing special time with your baby. Gone are the interruptions and distractions of your daytime existence. The undone chores do not tug at you at this hour; the older children are tucked into their beds. You are free to give your undivided attention to your baby.[4]

BEGIN BY NOT TURNING ON THE OVERHEAD LIGHT in the room where you will be feeding the baby. Sit in the dark or use a night light or a shaded lamp with a low-wattage bulb. Electric lighting is unsettling to the nervous system—yours and baby's. Sit in the same chair, a rocker or glider if you have one, every night. Play a soothing CD, lullabies perhaps or light classical music or meditative instrumentals.

Contemplate the miracle in your arms. You and your baby melt into a oneness of peaceful vibrations. You commune with each other. After the feeding, the baby, nourished in both body and spirit, drifts back to sleep wrapped in your silent epiphanies of love.

THE NEXT CEREMONY CAN BE DONE at any time of the year, but New Year's Eve is an especially auspicious occasion for Blessings and Burdens.[5] This uncomplicated ritual consists of writing two lists: one for the blessings that came your way during the past year, the other for the burdens that weighed you down over those same twelve months. At exactly midnight ceremoniously burn your burdens in an attractive, fireproof container. Watch as the flames devour your angers, terrors, and frustrations, transforming them into a little pile of gray ash. Spread the ashes outdoors, so that not even a speck of your burdens remains. As the ashes blow away, know that you are free to begin afresh. You have left the past in the past! Erasing your burdens once a year allows you to go forth without carrying the residue of emotion that naturally trails behind any misfortune.

The "blessings" list may be kept by your bed. Read it over at least once a week and give thanks. Your grateful heart increases the opportunity for yet more blessings to reach you.

THE THIRD CEREMONY CONCERNS CREATING A CONNECTION with Mother Nature.[6] Step outdoors onto a patch of earth. Close your eyes and imagine that you are a tree. Center your attention on your feet, feeling roots growing out of your soles into the dark earth. Raise your arms, visualizing your arms, hands, and fingers as tree branches. Connect with sky energy. Feel the wind moving your branches. Notice the rhythmic patterns your branches create against the blue sky.

Bring your attention to your feet again. Feel the green of the grass rising up in you and moving into your legs and spine, which are the tree's trunk. See the tree vividly with as much detail as possible. Breathe deeply, again and again. Become a column of living energy— green energy stretching out to the vast blueness of space. Inhale and start bringing the blue energy into you and exhale, from your tree- ness, green energy into the sky. With each breath you become a con- duit between earth and sky.

End by letting go of your treeness. In your mind's eye see yourself lying on the ground, looking up into the sky. You are now back to your ordinary dimensions, yet you remain a conduit of earth/sky energy. You end feeling revitalized by the subtle vigor of this tree visualization. Letting the natural world into your crowded life through meditation settles and composes you as you prepare to begin your day.

These three active meditations can be seen as variations on the theme of motherhood: mothering a child, mothering yourself, and being mothered by nature. The elemental matter *(mater)* of the universe—Water *(milk)*, Fire, Earth, and Sky—is the mother of us all.

5

THE SENSES: *Open wide the doors to the temple*

may you have rainbows

salmon tumbling upstream at dawn
deer pounding into a firestorm sunset
the beating of butterfly wings at noon
grassy hills with that late spring smell
oceans of sky on an august day
the silk of long-legged irises
a grape arbor at twilight   ripening

TAKEN COLLECTIVELY, the senses provide inroads to the soul. In addition, each one—sight, hearing, smell, touch, and taste—can stand alone as a profound blessing in its own right.

A *REFRIGERATOR ALTAR*[7] will awaken your vision with a mural of delight. Begin by decluttering the fridge door—remove the errand lists, the dry-cleaning receipt, the invitation to Aunt Sarah's eightieth birthday, the dog food coupons, the snapshots. Replace these sundry items with a few (no more than three) visual images that draw you within, where you are able to catch a glimpse of your real self hidden beneath the "doer," who tends to be constantly preoccupied with dashing hither and yon. Perhaps a photo of rocks smoothed by water instantly rescues you from the rush of your day. Or a picture of a summer sky cut from a magazine can visually say "Breathe!" as you feel an expanse of luminous blue filling your being. Or an inexpensive reproduction of your favorite artwork (sans mat and frame) can refresh you by capturing your attention with its beauty.

Consider how often you approach the refrigerator with food on your mind—before you open the door take a moment to nourish your soul.

THE TINY WIND CHIME[8] that caught your attention all summer because it was light enough to respond to the softest breeze need not be tucked away come the fall. Its mission during steamy summer days was to awaken your heart to gratitude for the slightest puff of air. Now, the garden wilts and frosts over; indoors it is cool enough to turn on the furnace. Hang the delicate wind chime near a heater vent. Whenever the heat comes on, a current of warm air will move the chimes; the tinkling sound will elicit a silent thank you for the blessing of heat, a luxury many are without as the cold begins to strengthen.

DAMPEN A COTTON HANKIE with your favorite essence oil.[9] Walk around the room waving the handkerchief. Move slowly, allowing the aroma to fill the expanse of the room, freshening stale air, and dispelling any negative vibrations. Your olfactory sense will delight in this simple meditative act that allows your spirit to rise.

WRITE ON THE HEART of mother earth the word "release" and call upon the purifying powers of the earth to free you of a burden you've carried too long.

Take a walk on a quiet beach before beginning this "letting go" ritual. When you feel ready, step to the tide line, bend down, and slowly write R-E-L-E-A-S-E with your index finger. Notice the feel of the wet sand as it gives way beneath the strong intent of your finger. Step back onto dry sand; watch the flow of waves cover the word; see the ebbing waves erase it, tugging your burden out to sea.[10] Allow the release to ease your mind.

Give back something to the ocean—a rock, a shell, a piece of driftwood. Toss it to the tides as a symbolic thank you.

THε NEXT TIMε ƴOU SIT DOWN to eat alone, close your eyes as you taste that very first bite. Chew slowly. Savor it. Wait until it is totally liquefied before swallowing. This meditation[II] becomes an act of grace that flavors your entire meal. Open your eyes and finish the remainder of your repast at your normal pace, but let it be a silent feast, sans television, radio, music, or reading. In the space the silence creates, the food's color, texture, and aroma become paramount. Enjoy!

THε SIXTH SεNSε MAƳ Bε LOCATεD somewhere between the heart and the pubic bone. It often manifests as a disturbing feeling in the belly. This wrench of foreboding in the gut can be accompanied by a mental flash as you see/feel the person or event at the center of your concern.

Remembering that "psychic" is derived from the Greek word "psyche," meaning soul, consider honoring your sixth sense rather than shrugging off your premonition. Select a symbol that calls to mind the person or event in question. Light a candle and meditatively imagine the light from that candle surrounding the symbol. Then, lift the candle and encircle the symbol by describing in the air a protective ring of light, using the candle flame. This small ritual allows you to express your foreboding in a positive way. Rather than suppressing your concern, you have transformed the darkness into light.

By working with your senses you open the passageways between the inner and outer worlds. As sensory blockages fall away, the inner self shines through.

6

The thresholds
of the day

early morning

long slender notes hang in the air of our room
my hands reach for the reed flute you played last night
from the hollow stalk I drink in your breath then
swallow it like wine

IN THE INTRICATE PATTERN of your busy schedule, when is there time to deepen? Any contemplative practice necessitates having an interval when you can be undisturbed while you seek the wisdom of your deeper self. Consider which time of day best allows you to dedicate ten to twenty minutes to meditation. Affirmation is the technique offered for each of these four meditations: dawn, noon, dusk, and midnight.

DAWN

Dawn creates the backdrop for a visual bond between your inner self and the rising sun.

AS *MORNING ARTICULATES THE DARK* recesses of the world, repeatedly sing (or silently say), "Light is incredibly generous."[12] From first light to sunrise is a magical time, since the mists of sleep obscure the tasks that await you after breakfast. Adrift on a timeless sea, you observe your inner self unveiled by the ever-increasing light. By singing (to a tune of your own choosing) that one-line mantra again and again,

you call to your inner light to rise up within your being. By the end of
the meditation the sun has risen, splashing colorful warmth every-
where. And your face emanates the glow of your shining center as
you move into your day.

NOON

Noon traditionally caters to the body, yet, just as easily, can be a time to
replenish the spirit.

CLEAR ANY CLUTTER FROM THE KITCHEN TABLE and wipe it clean. In the
center, place a sunshine yellow candle, a bag of uncooked beans, and
a ceramic bowl. As you light the candle, thank the sun for its role in
bringing the bean crop to maturation. Gather foods you will be eating for lunch and place them in a circle around the candle. Chant (or
say silently to yourself) the affirmation, "I am provided for."[13] To
chant, simply intone the words in a droning voice. Let each repetition
be a thank you to all beings responsible for bringing this meal to your
table. Begin with the farmer, and imagine the entire sequence of

people up to and including the bagger at the supermarket. Let your affirmation broadcast your gratitude to each link in the human chain. Ceremoniously pour the beans into the bowl; their clacking sound creates a testament to the blessings in your life.

This abundance bowl is never depleted—each noon you pour the same beans into the same bowl, and chant the same "I am provided for" mantra as an offering of thanks to all who make each day's noon meal possible. This symbolic food is never cooked; instead, it is returned to the bag to await the next day's pouring ritual. The abundance bowl becomes a part of your noon meal; with a little practice the ritual takes only minutes to perform and adds a spiritual note to your lunchtime break.

DUSK

Darkness seeps into the day sky like a piece of dyed cloth bleeding into rinse water. This is the time of two lights: dusk, the shadow catcher, gathers the darkness until daycolors disappear in the soft underness of night.

SLIP INTO THE CRACK BETWEEN THE DAY WORLD and the night realm. Step outdoors and silently repeat this affirmation, "I still my thoughts until the quietness of the earth wraps me in its heavy cotton."[14] Let the tensions of the day drain out the soles of your feet, as you repeat this mantra to the exclusion of all other thoughts. When you feel that your mind is quiet, reenter your home, enriched and refreshed through your contact with nature.

MIDNIGHT

The atmosphere of midnight steals over you like the distant hoot of an owl. The midnight hour gives you the gift of an expanse of time in which to bless yourself and your loved ones. At times, you may find yourself obsessively worrying over someone. One positive affirmation for a friend or relative who is suffering through a difficult time is, "There are so many ways for things to get better"[15]. Try writing this mantra as you repeat it aloud or say it silently. The physical act of writing will calm you; each time you write the sentence, envision yet one more way in which the worrisome situation could improve. This may seem like wishful thinking, but the mind is a powerful tool, and applying the balm of positive thought carries a healing vibration to all concerned.

Any of these affirmations may be repeated silently at any time of day or night—it is a way to dip into the well of spirit that is always present within.

7

How the ever-changing seasons affect your contemplative spirit

seasonals

the milky way
rolled out like a bolt of silk
pales into
cold morning
            *
strings of bees
hum exultation
blackbird shimmers
raku-fire
            *

peachblossoms
float on the pond
Buddha breathes
waterlilies
            *
at the shrine
chrysanthemums
strewn on the grass
sticks for I Ching

SMALL GESTURES offer respectful attention to the connection between the seasons of nature and those of the human heart. These simple ceremonies are known as "earth rites."

WINTER

The primal wild wind of winter drives you inward to the still point at the center of your being, where deep silence abounds. Winter is the midnight time of the soul, when you listen for the wisdom within.

LIGHT A COLLECTION OF CANDLES, or sit before a hearth fire; in the winter's long dark, firelight enlivens you with its warmth and energy. Place your lightly crossed hands over the center of your chest, or place your hands in a prayer pose, pressing the backs of the thumbs to your breastbone. Listen to the pulse of your being, the center of your bodily universe. Let that "thu-thump" be the only sound. When thoughts intrude on your listening, your heartbeat vanishes. Gently return your focus to the sound at your core. Be one with the heart rhythm as you hear/feel its pulse in your fingers and palms. Unbidden thoughts may interrupt again; allow your mind to release its meanderings, and center once more on the pulse of your heart. This meditation provides a balm for winter doldrums.

To conclude the meditation, bow to the flames, outward symbols of the heart's inner fire. With every rhythmic pulsation this hollow, muscular organ circulates your lifeblood. The miracle of existence moves just beneath the surface of your awareness. Whisper a thank you to the universal life force and to the heart that allows you to touch the place of wisdom alive in the intervals between the beats.

SPRING

The urgent cravings of spring can be felt in the softening wind, in the stirring of songbirds, in the bravery of crocus and snowdrop, in the vulnerability of tree buds, maiden fernheads, and daffodil shoots.

THIS SEASONAL MEDITATION appears deceptively simple, yet beneath its veneer lies a delicate attunement between your inner spirit and the universal soul of nature.

Step outdoors. Discover from which direction the wind is blowing. Face into the wind. Be aware of the wind in your hair, on your face, against your clothing. Lift your arms overhead and feel the wind

on your palms. Scoop the air into your hands and swoosh it over your body down to your toes. Continue the stretching and bending of this rite of spring, feeling that you are bathing yourself in the clarity of fresh air.

Now come to a standstill. The gentle exertion of your movements has deepened your breathing. Close your eyes, and let your breath and the spring breeze move in concert with each other. The breeze breathes for you; every pore is open; the wind moves through you— winter cobwebs disappear. Spring, the season of conceiving, of quickening, of birthing, offers you the opportunity to start afresh. You are cleansed of winter's residue—let your heart speak to you of its dreams for the coming year. Choose one; then resolve "by the power of the wind" to pursue a course that will uphold the wings of your dream. The dream is never enough—you must act in accordance with your heart's desire if it is ever to bear fruit. The clear-mindedness of this meditation helps you not only to see the path, but also to choose to walk it.

SUMMER

The thrown-wide window of summer lets in all that is lush, sensuous, fragrant. Summer heat slows the harried pace. The long light of the season provides a backdrop for sunrise walks, lunches "al fresco," and evening swims. Summertime fosters an easy connection between your inner self and the flourishing earth, although a slight shift of consciousness is necessary to connect your interior sacred space with summer's fecundity.

BEGIN THE MEDITATION BY PLACING A ROSE, or other summer flower, a pair of scissors, and a glass of water before you. Breathe in as if you were sipping air in through a straw; exhale through closed lips with a hum. While gazing at the flower, continue this "sipping breath," each time following it with a gentle "m-m-m-m-m." With each round, permit yourself to become one with the flower's shape, color, petals, stem, leaves. Through this meditation you are becoming a gardener of the spirit, imbibing the abundance, fragrance, and fertility of summer. Your exhalations mimic the drone of bumblebees, honeybees, hummingbirds.

When the wilting heat of summer saps your energies, this ritual provides a way to renew inner wellsprings of vitality. End this contemplation by taking a few swallows of water—a way of honoring summer's most precious element. Then, snip the bottom of the flower's stem and plunge it into the glass for a needed drink. Place the flower on your bedside table so it is the last sight you glimpse at night and the first to greet you in the morning.

AUTUMN

Autumn bathes the earth in a honey light. Yet as the season descends toward the edge of winter, the vivid colors of early fall soften to ochre, umber, sienna. The falling down sun drapes mother earth in a light more bronze than gold. Earth offers up her bounty beneath a diminished sun; the last of the harvest pulled in before it is lost to a white chill—grapes for wine, apples for sauce, pumpkins for pie.

As the focal point for a fall contemplation, create an autumnal altar.[16] Gather miniature pumpkins, gourds, squashes together with sprays of bittersweet, cuttings of ivy, mums, asters, pomegranates, and grapes. Let this display of plenty symbolize the many blessings in your life.

Light one candle to represent your grateful heart, and place it in the midst of the abundance. Center your attention on your breath. Exhale, then wait for your breath to find you. After a certain interval, air comes in through your nostrils once more. Then, it goes out. Be passive. You are not inhaling, rather you are watching for the return of your breath. There is no need to do anything except keep a vigil by continually witnessing the receptive pause between out-breath and in-breath. Each time the breath finds its way in, let it fill your heart with gratitude. When your interval of thanksgiving feels complete, end with a bow to the harvest.

Through this breath meditation you have connected deeply with the earth's autumnal energy. At this juncture mother earth is spent. She suspends activity for the winter months, waiting and watching for the increase of light which will herald spring stirrings. In the same manner that your warm breath found you, the strengthening vernal sun will find her. Listen, come springtime, for that first inhalation!

8

Meditations to inspire

just past full

round

    orange

        delicious

            melting

               moon

IF YOU HAVE OFTEN DREAMED of treading the artist's path but have resisted the urge to take the first step, consider this question: "What artistic endeavor would you pursue if you were assured, in advance, that you could not fail?" Take a few minutes to contemplate this question before reading further.

Removing failure from the equation helps you clarify your dreams, since everyone feels a bit unsure about unveiling the authentic self beneath the personality's veneer. Your inner being is "on display," and, understandably, you feel vulnerable.

Once you have acknowledged the depth and breadth of your artistic dream, the next step is to center on ways to open creative pathways to the deep mind, source of all creative energy. The first active meditation creates the impetus for an artistic undertaking by fueling that initial burst of inspiration.

GATHER TOGETHER A SMALL PAD of paper, a pen, a cutting board, a knife, a wide-mouthed glass, and two or three oranges. Light a candle and/or play a CD that inspires you. Very slowly lift one orange, hold it up to the light. Note its parrot's beak color, its cratered skin, its aroma. Place it on the cutting board and meditatively slice it in two. Experience the cutting sounds, the juice running before the knife, the white fibers and seeds against the flesh. Squeeze both halves into the glass; see the juice drip, its color sliding down the clear sides. Say aloud, "Beneath the skin of my surface mind lies the juice of creativity."

Repeat these steps with all the oranges. Ceremoniously drink the juice, feeling its tang opening your creative pathways. The meditative pace of this exercise[17] keeps you centered in the here and now, thus bypassing your logical mind with its inhibiting excuses and doubts. To end, jot down your reactions to this meditation; keep the pen and small pad in your pocket or purse—a sure way to pin down creative promptings before they slip away.

THE DEEP MIND IS ALWAYS AWAKE, aware, alert. If you find yourself creatively blocked, know that the obstacles lie in your surface mind, with its constant chatter about the mundane world. The following is a way to startle your conscious mind into momentary silence, long enough for you to dive deep to the source of all creativity, the spiritual center of your being.

When you first arise in the morning, prior to showering, sit before a large bowl, three-quarters full of cold water. Stand a mirror behind the bowl, and place a face towel beside it. Dip your whole face in the bowl three separate times. After the third time, look at yourself in the mirror and say, "I am diving deep and recapturing the stimulating flow of creative ideas." Only then pat your face dry.

No matter how the conscious mind tries to intellectualize this experience beforehand, the physical fact of cold water against warm flesh will surprise it into silence. In that silence lies your opportunity to connect with your deeper self. As you push your face through the surface of the water, you are pushing through creative blocks.

WHEN YOU HAVE COMPLETED A CREATIVE PROJECT, the tendency is to rush into a new artistic endeavor. Instead, consider giving your artwork its moment in the sun. Place your artwork—photo, pottery, sheet music, poem, needlepoint, painting—on a table in your living room. Toast your work with champagne or sparkling grape juice. Then, ceremoniously bring in three gifts for the muse—that inspiring force in your inner life. The gifts are in another room, so each time you are about to reenter the living room, pause and think, "I cross the threshold into artistic completion, bearing a gift of gratitude for my muse." Place the gifts—perhaps a flower, a piece of fruit, a lit candle—on the table with your artwork. End by taking a photo of this arrangement, so you can often contemplate who you are in the light of what you have created. The creative self partners with the muse and art appears.

These three rituals correspond to three distinct phases in the creative process: inception, deadlock, completion. However, any of them can be used whenever you need to replenish creative vitality. Active meditation always invigorates the artistic imagination and so provides the perfect antidote to burnout.

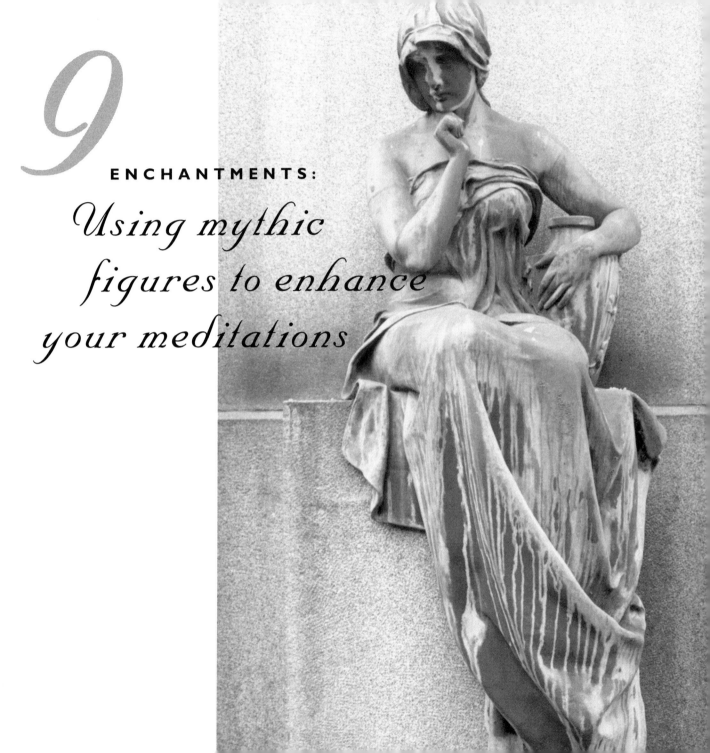

9

ENCHANTMENTS:

Using mythic figures to enhance your meditations

the goddess speaks to a temple dancer

dance for
dance for no one
dance for no one other
dance for no one other than
dance for no one other than yourself
and

      all the women
      all the women who
      all the women who lost
      all the women who lost the rhythm
      all the women who lost the rhythm of the steps then

forgot they ever knew
               how to dance
dance for them
        lady, dance!
dance for them
        dance!

UNFOLD YOUR INNER SELF by creating an active meditation that evolves from a favorite myth, fairy tale, folk story, religious parable, fable, or legend. Who came to mind as you read this last sentence? Often it is wise to embrace the first character who darts into your mind before you have even a moment to defend against this flash of intuition! Whoever slipped by the guardian at the gate of your conscious mind embodies an aggregate of vital energy—a gift from your deeper self.

PREPARE TO "BECOME" this mythic figure by choosing clothing, hair ornaments, or jewelry which symbolizes your chosen persona. (Chapter II lists a full array of options.) This meditation allows you an opportunity to penetrate the mystery realm of the unconscious and acquire a fuller portrait of yourself. The act of witnessing your hidden aspects creates a rebalancing on the conscious level, as you unfold a more complex view of yourself.

Once you have chosen a persona, select an accoutrement that manifests the intrinsic feel of this character. A large filmy scarf is quite versatile. It can be a veil that covers your head and face while you turn within to seek the counsel of your mythic counterpart, or you might wrap your whole body in it to symbolize engulfing yourself in the protective energies of this archetypal personage; twist the veil around your head, forming a turban that signifies the honor you bestow on this figure; roll the scarf into a narrow sash, encircling your waist and thus girding yourself with the power and authority of this legendary figure; throw the veil over your shoulders, and it becomes a cape symbolizing the majesty of your alter ego; for a medieval flavor, place the scarf on your head (leaving your face free), and secure it with a headband, wreath of ivy, or circlet of flowers.

Once you have adorned yourself, sit before a mirror, light a candle, and become the character. Whether she be goddess, witch, heroine, magician, priestess, or anyone else, see yourself transformed. Listen meditatively, watching and waiting for the character to "speak" through gesture, facial expression, inner monologue, or movement.

This meditation need not be long (five to twenty minutes). When you feel that you've penetrated the mystery gift of this persona, bow to your reflection in the mirror and contemplate the manner in which this archetypal person relates to your current life. Take time to integrate any wisdom shared by your mythic self. You have been attracted to this character because she resounds with a deep aspect of your psyche that needs to be made manifest. Ask for her blessing. Extinguish the candle. Know that, through meditation, you have imbued the article of ornamentation with a contagious energy. From this point forward, it will have a stimulating effect on your deeper mind whenever you wear it for an active meditation. If you wish, you might display this special accoutrement in a place of honor in your bedroom, welcoming it into your dreams.

10

ECHOES: *Consecrating everyday actions*

shrine

temple bell
  fills me
with sound
  empty moon

ONCE YOU HAVE EXPERIMENTED with a few active meditations, you may find yourself searching for small, simple rituals to sprinkle throughout your day. In the beginning choose one and stay with that practice for one month, giving it ample time to become part of your routine.

THERE ARE MANY POSSIBILITIES in the realm of one-minute-or-less meditations. For instance, you might consider placing a small bell in the back seat of your car. As you drive around corners, or stop short, the bell will get jostled and ring. When you hear it ring, notice the nature of your thoughts at the moment you hear the sound[18]. Look at who or what is in your thoughts.

Over time, the technique helps you become aware of your thought patterns: mental meanderings, obsessions, worries, pleasures, and daydreams. The simple act of mentally stepping back and observing your thoughts creates a space between you and them. Thoughts that are observed lose their grip on your mind, setting you free to *choose* what you wish to dwell on. Within a few minutes your mind may well return to its obsessive behavior, but the bell will ring again and you will be given yet another occasion to bear witness to this awareness: the thoughts are not the mind—the mind is sky, the thoughts are clouds that come and go, puff up and thin out, turn dark and roiling, only to be replaced by huge billows of soft white. The clouds float by. The sky remains unchanged.

Aside from listening to the silence behind the chatter of your thoughts, other meditations include listening to recordings of calming music or poetry. When you are listening to these CDs as background, spend one minute sitting quietly and actually hearing the music or the poetry. Let the sounds be your focal point for a full minute, thereby chasing your thoughts away as you center on the notes or words to the exclusion of all else.

ANOTHER SIXTY-SECOND LISTENING MEDITATION: Throw open a window and still your thoughts by attending to the twittering of song sparrows, the lapping of lake water, the sound of wind in branches. Pay attention to the mewling of kittens lying on the sunny porch, curled against their mother. Small nature breaks refresh your spirit and renew your energy.

If you are able to take a twenty-minute walk each day, you might pause for a minute during the walk to contemplate nature. The thoughts that play continuously in your mind tend to accompany you on your walk. So, pause for a few moments during the walk to contemplatively pick some wild flowers, sprinkle a pocketful of birdseed near a favorite tree, or squat down and place your hands in a fast-moving stream. Any attunement with nature quiets your thoughts.

THE FINAL LESS-THAN-A-MINUTE MEDITATION is a silent or vocal food blessing. Place your hands, palms down, above your plate of food and say a thank you to the powers that be. Leave your hands in place for a few moments, breathe in the aroma of your food, then murmur, "All is holy . . . my body, my garden, my food."

All of the active meditations in this chapter offer opportunities to express your reverence for spirit through the addition of short ceremonies in the course of your daily life.

11

Create your own
active meditations

rosary

her body the wine
ripe in drown voices
at this depth her spins
magic our mouth
with spill-roses
into ritual sundays
the grotto her harvest
our recite of firewater
virgins the poetic
along the black seine
mother of the ellipse
rivers where we sit
unto goddess

USING THIS SUMMARY SECTION you can create your own active meditation by selecting at least one item from each list and combining them in a creative way. Here's an example:

The intent of this meditative act is seeing the sacred in ordinary existence (list 1). While you are filling the kettle or coffee pot from the tap, let the sight and sound of running water (list 2) center you. When the coffee is ready, spend a few moments enjoying the steamy aroma (list 3). Before taking that first delicious sip, walk to a window and lift your cup toward the morning sun, welcoming the light and the new day.

I. *Intentions for active meditations*

Celebration

Fertility

Devotion

Offerings

Healing

Protection

Blessing

Mourning

Honoring your ancestors

Clearing your mind

Changing the vibrations

Harvests

Rites of passage

Naming ceremony

Acknowledging seasonal change

Performance art

Seeing the sacred in ordinary existence

Connecting with universal energy

Honoring an interrelatedness with the planet

Discovering the spiritual in a daily task

Sparking the creative muse

II.

"Props" to use for an active meditation
(Props can be the real thing, or a painting or photo of it.)

ELEMENTS

Air:
Angels
Wings
Clouds
Flag
Windsock
Wind in the trees
Birds
Butterflies
Veils
Scarves
Sailboats
Fireplace bellows
Feathers
Open window

Fire:
Incense
Smudge stick
Candle
Hearth
Lightning
Sun
Campfire
Torch
Kiln
Phoenix

Water:
Running tap
Glass bowl of spring water
Ocean
River
Lake
Pond
Stream
Rain
Mirror

Earth:
Rocks
Stones
Crystals
Plants
Trees
Flowers
Mountains
Cornucopia
Fruits
Vegetables
Dry rice, dry beans, and so on
Bowl of potting soil

III. *Methods of focusing during an active meditation*

SENSES

Smelling (incense, flowers, fruit, herbs, sweetgrass)

Tasting (foods, salt, herbs, water, wine, milk, honey)

Touching (fabrics, stones, trees, water)

Gazing (candles, horizon, body of water)

Listening (music, chanting, songs, nature sounds)

Immersing your hands or face in a bowl of water

Smudging

Playing an instrument

Creating an altar[19]

Mimicking an animal

MOVEMENT

Dance

Gesture

Crossing thresholds

Walking in procession

Meditative walking

Tai Chi

Yoga

Wearing symbolic clothing, jewelry, veils, scarves, hair ornaments, and so on

CLASSIC MEDITATION FOCAL POINTS

Heartbeat

Breath

Guided imagery

Inner light

Mantra

Candlegazing

IV. *Ornamentation (optional in creating active meditations)*

HAIR

Flowers

Wreaths of herbs, ivy, flowers

Headband

Barrette

Hair clips

Beads

Braids with a ribbon entwined

Headdress

SKIN

Perfume

Essence oil

Makeup

Body paint

Henna tattoos

CLOTHING ACCESSORIES

Scarves

Shawls

Vest

Belt

Tunic

Poncho

JEWELRY

Rings

Toe rings

Anklets

Bracelets

Necklaces

Earrings

CEREMONIAL CLOTHING

Any skirt, shirt, dress, or pants that has meaning due to:

Color

Fabric

Country of origin

Person who gave it to you

Design depicted on it

Notes

1. Sophy Burnham, *A Book of Angels*, New York: Ballantine Books, 1990, pp. 223-226.

2. This ritual was shared by fine artist and close friend, Christine King.

3. The six listed purifications were offered by Karen Tripp, RNC, LMT, Clinical Aromatherapist/Reflexologist, Aroma Therapy Bodywork Co., 560 Tremont St., Dighton, MA 02715, (508) 880-3777.

4. This meditation was shared by my daughter, Cara A. C. Garretson, journalist and new mother.

5. Mary Elizabeth Peterson offered this ritual. She is the mother of twins and a professional artist who finds her inspiration in nature. She can be reached at mattandmary1@comcast.net.

6. Shared by Linda Hogan, Shamanic Healer/Reiki Practitioner, Wild Women Enterprises, 2 Douglas Pike, Smithfield, RI, (401) 949-0049, *www.wildwomen-ent.com.*

7. This idea was shared by Mary Elizabeth Peterson.

8. This idea was given to me by Denise Geddes, photographer and wonderful friend, collaborator, and soul-sister!

9. This ritual was offered by Karen Tripp.

10 This meditation was shared by photographer Denise Geddes. It may also be done in your garden, using a hose to erase letters, one by one. Then, bury a small gift for the earth in your garden.

11 Bernard Gunther, *What to Do till the Messiah Comes* (New York: Collier Books, 1971), p. 32.

12 John O'Donohue, *Anam Cara* (New York: HarperCollins Publishers, 1997), p. 1.

13 This affirmation was shared by fine artist J. B. Kay, *www.danky.com/coachjbk* or *www.danky.com/jbkartworks*.

14 Michael Dorris, *Morning Girl* (New York: Hyperion Books for Children, 1992), p. 26.

15 Amy Tan, *The Joy Luck Club* (New York: Ivy Books, 1989), p. 141.

16 For an in-depth view of the art of altar creation consult *A Book of Women's Altars* by Nancy Brady Cunningham and Denise Geddes (York Beach, ME: Red Wheel/Weiser, 2002).

17 The seed idea for this active meditation can be found in *What to Do till the Messiah Comes* by Bernard Gunther.

18 This technique is taught by yoga teacher and friend, Charlotte Waterman.

19 Cunningham and Geddes, *A Book of Women's Altars*.

Bibliography

Bender, Sue. *Everyday Sacred*. New York: HarperCollins Publishers, 1995.

Boice, Judith, ed. *Mother Earth*. San Francisco: Sierra Club Books, 1992.

Budapest, Z. *The Grandmother of Time*. New York: Harper and Row Publishers Inc., 1979.

Conway, D. J. *A Little Book of Altar Magic*. Freedom, CA: Crossing Press, 2000.

Cuhulain, Kerr. *Wiccan Warrior*. St. Paul: Llewellyn Publications, 2001.

Cunningham, Nancy Brady and Denise Geddes. *A Book of Women's Altars*. York Beach, ME: Red Wheel/Weiser, 2002.

Dorris, Michael. *Morning Girl*. New York: Hyperion Books for Children, 1992.

Drake, Michael. *The Shamanic Drum*. Bend, OR: Talking Drum Publications, 1991.

Gorman, Clem. *The Book of Ceremony*. Cambridge, England: Whole Earth Tools, 1972.

Gunther, Bernard. *What to Do till the Messiah Comes*. New York: Collier Books, 1971.

Harp, David. *The Three Minute Meditator*. San Francisco: Mind's I Press, 1987.

Monaghan, Patricia. *Wild Girls*. St. Paul: Llewellyn, 2001.

O'Donohue, John. *Anam Cara*. New York: HarperCollins Publishers, 1997.

Starhawk. *The Spiral Dance*. New York: Harper and Row Publishers Inc., 1979.

Stewart, Iris J. *Sacred Woman, Sacred Dance*. Rochester, VT: Inner Traditions, 2000.

Resources

CDs

Bachman, Alan Scott. *Kali Ma: Dances of Transformation*. Desert Wind, P.O. Box 3722, Salt Lake City, UT 84110

Carol, Shawna. *Goddess Chant*. Ladyslipper Inc., P.O. Box 3124, Durham, NC 27715

Premal, Deva. *The Essence*. Sounds True, P.O. Box 8010, Boulder, CO 80306

Redmond, Layne. *Chanting the Chakras: Roots of Awakening*. Sacred Source, P.O. Box 163, Crozet, VA 22932

World Music for Little Ears: Authentic Lullabies from around the World. Ellipsis Arts, P.O. Box 305, Roslyn, NY 11576

VIDEO

Rumi: Poet of the Heart, featuring Coleman Barks. Magnolia Films, P.O. Box 2998, San Anselmo, CA 94979

PILGRIMAGES/STUDY TOURS FOR WOMEN

Goddess Pilgrimage to Crete with Carol Christ and Sacred Journey in Greece* with Carol Christ.

Contact: Ariadne Institute for the Study of Myth and Ritual, Ltd., P.O. Box 791596, New Orleans, LA, 70179-1596 Tel: (504) 486-9119 Email: *institute@goddessariadne.org* Web site: *www.goddessariadne.org*

*Nancy Brady Cunningham attended the pilgrimage to Lesbos in 1999. The days were filled with women's rituals, including dance, yoga, poetry, and art—a moving and sacred experience!

About the Author and the Photographer

Nancy Brady Cunningham has been a yoga, meditation, and women's ritual leader for more than thirty years. Also an accomplished poet, she is the author of *I Am Woman by Rite: A Book of Women's Rituals*, *A Book of Women's Altars*, and coauthor of *Tarot Celebrations*.

Denise Geddes is a photography teacher in Massachusetts. Her photographs have appeared in *Free at Last*, *Tarot Celebrations*, *A Book of Women's Altars*, and *Song of the Beech Tree*.

To Our Readers

Red Wheel, an imprint of Red Wheel/Weiser, publishes books on topics ranging from spunky self-help, spirituality, personal growth, and relationships to women's issues and social issues. Our mission is to publish quality books that will make a difference in people's lives—how we feel about ourselves and how we relate to one another and to the world at large. We value integrity, compassion, and receptivity, both in the books we publish and in the way we do business.

Our readers are our most important resource, and we value your input, suggestions, and ideas about what you would like to see published. Please feel free to contact us, to request our latest book catalog, or to be added to our mailing list.

Red Wheel/Weiser, LLC
P.O. Box 612
York Beach, ME 03910-0612
www.redwheelweiser.com